ESSENTIAL **DK** MANAGERS

WRITING YOUR
RESUMÉ

SIMON HOWARD

DK

DK PUBLISHING, INC.

A DK PUBLISHING BOOK
www.dk.com

Editor Gwen Edmonds
Designer Laura Watson
US Editor Gary Werner

DTP Designer Jason Little
Production Controller Silvia La Greca

Senior Editor Adèle Hayward
Senior Designer Tassy King

Managing Editors Stephanie Jackson,
Jonathan Metcalf
Managing Art Editor Nigel Duffield

First American Edition, 1999
2 4 6 8 10 9 7 5 3 1

Published in the United States by
DK Publishing Inc., 375 Hudson Street,
New York, New York 10014

DK Publishing books are available at special
discounts for bulk purchases for sales promotions
or premiums. Special editions, including
personalized covers, excerpts of existing guides,
and corporate imprints can be created in large
quantities for specific needs. For more information,
contact Special Markets Dept./DK Publishing, Inc./375
Hudson Street/New York, NY 10014/Fax: 800-600-
9098

Library of Congress Cataloging-in-Publication Data

Howard, Simon
   Writing your resumé / by Simon Howard --
1st American ed.
      p.   cm. -- (Essential managers)
   Includes index.
   ISBN-13: 978-0-7894-4860-6 (alk.paper)
   ISBN-10: 0-7894-4860-2 (alk.paper)
   1. Résumé (Employment) I. Title. II. Series.
HF5383.S543 1999
808'.06665--dc21   99-15778
                                                  CIP

Reproduced by Colourscan, Singapore
Printed in China by WKT Company Limited

CONTENTS

CREATING YOUR RESUMÉ

PUTTING YOUR RESUMÉ TOGETHER

USING YOUR RESUMÉ

INTRODUCTION

We live in an age in which we are all increasingly responsible for the development of our own careers. In the changing world of work, our resumé is our passport to new opportunities, and consequently it is the most important career document we ever produce. There is no "right way" to create a perfect resumé – we are all individuals and our resumés will all be different. Writing Your Resumé helps you to identify your uniqueness and guides you through planning, creating, and using your resumé. It will cause you to think about your attributes as a person, your skills as a professional, and your hopes for the future. Full of practical information, exercises, and 101 invaluable tips, this book will help you to produce a resumé that is perfect for you.

PLANNING YOUR RESUMÉ

Your resumé is a brochure, not an autobiography. Its purpose is to help you in the process of finding a new job by selling your skills and experience to the right person.

UNDERSTANDING RESUMÉS

Before you start compiling your resumé, you need to familiarize yourself with the few basic rules of resumé construction. Everyone is different, and so are their resumés. However, the basic principles of what will produce a good end result remain the same.

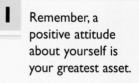

1 Remember, a positive attitude about yourself is your greatest asset.

CULTURAL DIFFERENCES

There are many conventions about resumés around the world. In the US, a one-page resumé is standard, while in continental Europe, many employers would expect a four- or five-page resumé that includes detailed information on educational achievements and professional qualifications.

WHAT IS A RESUMÉ?

A resumé is a professional marketing tool. It is the initial means by which you "sell" your skills. Its sole purpose is to provide sufficient information for prospective employers (or their agents) to register interest in you. There is more than one type of resumé, and you need to decide which of these is the most appropriate for you. Your aim is to produce a resumé that gets you to the next stage of the recruitment process; this may be an application form, an informal meeting, a telephone interview, or a formal interview.

UNDERSTANDING THE PRINCIPAL TYPES OF RESUMÉ

TYPE	USE
CHRONOLOGICAL Lists your employment history in reverse chronological order.	Most effective when you are applying for jobs in the same line of work and your resumé demonstrates a clear record of career progression.
FUNCTIONAL Highlights your principal skills and strengths rather than career history.	Most useful for first-time job hunters and those seeking a change of career direction, as the emphasis is not on career history but on transferable skills.
ONE-PAGE SUMMARY Summarizes your career and displays your track record.	Most effective for senior managers or those looking for freelance or temporary work. May be specifically requested by headhunters or employers.

CREATING A BROCHURE

The principal role of a resumé is to highlight your value to a potential employer, and to do that you must promote yourself. A document that is just a career summary will not sell the skills and attributes you have to offer. Your resumé needs to be a sales document – think of it as your career brochure. Consider those brochures that are most appealing: they are always well laid out, succinct, and easy to understand. The content of your resumé should inform the reader about you and your career. If that resumé is also clearly presented and 100 percent error-free, it will say a lot about your motivation and focus.

▲ **SETTING THE INTERVIEW AGENDA**
The usual purpose of your resumé is to earn you an interview. If you are selected for the interview, it will probably be your resumé that sets the agenda for that important initial meeting.

2 Set aside enough time to prepare and revise your resumé – it cannot be done in a single evening.

SETTING OBJECTIVES

The more focused your objectives, the more successful your resumé is likely to be. Identify those things that you have found fulfilling in order to help you be clear about future career goals, then analyze where you are now and where you want to go.

3 Remember, your career objectives will not be the same as others'.

4 Learn lessons from past experiences to use in the future.

LEARNING FROM ▼ YOUR EXPERIENCE

Plot a simple chart to put your career in perspective – it will help to show you what to look for in a new job.

ANALYZING YOUR CAREER

Everyone has their own set of career expectations. For some, progress will mean upward progression to more senior roles. Others will be looking for their work to fit in with a particular lifestyle. Whatever your priorities, your career will have consisted of a series of "career highs" and "career lows." Identify those highs and lows to analyze your progress beyond the qualifications and experience you have gained.

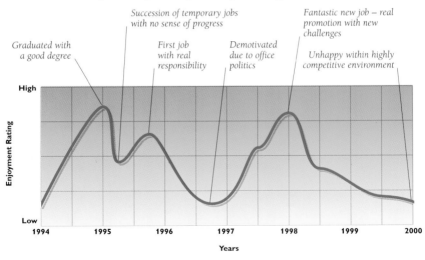

Graduated with a good degree

Succession of temporary jobs with no sense of progress

First job with real responsibility

Demotivated due to office politics

Fantastic new job – real promotion with new challenges

Unhappy within highly competitive environment

Enjoyment Rating

High

Low

1994 1995 1996 1997 1998 1999 2000

Years

DECIDING ON PRIORITIES

Learning from the past is important for all career seekers. Your analysis of career highs and lows will help you to identify the features of your past experience that you will want to find in a future career move. Some may be features that relate directly to the job, such as "to become head of department" or the location of the company. Others will be more subtle, such as "to feel comfortable with the team culture." Having identified these features, you must decide which are essential and which are desirable. Only you can decide on the priorities for your next move, but a clear list of objectives will help you judge any future job offers.

5 Be prepared to review and revise your objectives.

6 Be positive about what you can achieve in the future.

LISTING YOUR ▶ OBJECTIVES

Only you can decide which of your objectives are essential – those elements a future job must have – and which are just desirable.

Be clear about what really is essential to you

Be aware that lifestyle considerations will change at different stages in your working life

ESSENTIAL

Job related: Report to board level. Have control of project budgets. Run team of at least 8 people.

Lifestyle: Commute time of less than 30 minutes. No weekend traveling.

DESIRABLE

Job related: Be involved in new business development. Receive training in the latest technology.

Lifestyle: Be in walking distance of shops/cafes, etc. Have some flexibility of working hours.

7 Identify your career objectives, but include only your immediate aim in your resumé.

DO'S AND DON'TS

☑ Do look at friends' and colleagues' resumés, if they are willing.

☑ Do be honest about aspects of work you do not enjoy.

☑ Do talk to others about their goals.

☒ Don't set unrealistic targets – you will be disappointed.

☒ Don't belittle your achievements or expertise.

☒ Don't set yourself negative objectives.

9

FINDING YOUR NEXT JOB

Before you set out on your job search, you need to be aware of the methods you can use for securing a job. There are four main routes – it is important that you do not rely too much on just one of them, but explore the potential of each route for you.

8 When possible, send your job application to a named person.

9 Always quote any reference numbers when replying to job advertisements.

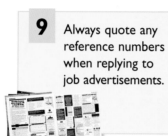

REPLYING TO JOB ADVERTISEMENTS

Employers and recruitment companies place many thousands of job advertisements every year. Through newspapers, professional magazines and journals, the Internet, and career fairs, applications are constantly sought. This is the most open and accessible market for jobs – and so the most competitive, but at least you know that employers who advertise are committed to recruiting.

CONTACTING RECRUITMENT COMPANIES

In general, recruitment companies find people for jobs, not jobs for people. Employers pay them a fee to provide qualified candidates, who can then be shortlisted for final selection. Although they rely on job seekers' resumés to make money, the service they provide to the job seeker varies enormously. There are two types of recruitment companies. The first type are those that operate databases, and these are often known as recruitment agencies. They range from the well-known general agencies through to firms specializing in professional or functional areas, such as finance or IT. Second, there are the search and selection companies who advertise or headhunt for individual posts. Both are important for the experienced job seeker.

THINGS TO DO

1. Make a note of which days the media advertise jobs relevant to you.
2. Search the Internet for useful recruitment and corporate sites.
3. Talk to colleagues about recruitment companies they can recommend.
4. Identify any trade events worth attending.
5. Monitor the press for companies that might be expanding.

JOB ADVERTISEMENT
The most open and
competitive route

RECRUITMENT COMPANY
A good route for people
with some experience

JOB SEEKER

SPECULATIVE APPLICATION
The least certain route
– requires a campaign

NETWORKING
The route open to
everyone at all levels

JOB
OFFER

▲ CONSIDERING ROUTES
*Whatever your current experience and
ambitions, all four routes should be
considered. Any one could yield a job.*

| **10** | Be methodical – it may take months to find a new job. |

MAKING SPECULATIVE APPLICATIONS

Personnel departments will receive a steady stream
of enquiries for what will be a limited number
of vacancies. However, if you have a clear idea of
what you want to do and who you want to do it
for, contacting employers directly can be effective.
The key is to contact the right person with a clear
proposition. Although a company may hold you in
their database, keep monitoring job advertisements.

NETWORKING

Someone you know knows someone who is
recruiting. Through your range of personal and
business contacts you can network to find your
next job. However, you will have to be open with
this route – to network successfully you need to
tell people, discreetly, that you are looking for a job.
It may be time-consuming, but for those starting
out or returning to work, it can be very effective.

| **11** | Make sure any networking you do to find a new job is discreet. |

11

DECIDING ON YOUR STRATEGY

Unfortunately, when searching for a new job, you cannot simply produce one perfect resumé. Your approach to every advertisement, recruitment company, and employer should be tailor-made to their specific requirements.

> **12** Always consider who the likely reader of your resumé will be.

CHOOSING THE RIGHT APPROACH

No two careers will be the same, so no two resumés will be the same, and no two career searches will be the same. It may be that you feel that there is more than one direction your career could take – you could choose to specialize in your own field or move into a more generalist managerial position. For different routes you will need to use different strategies, focusing on different skills and achievements. Whatever your next step, assess the tactics most likely to be successful.

ADAPTING A RESUMÉ ▶

The two directions in which this financial director can see her career progressing require different resumés and approaches. Highlight different skills and experience according to the type of application.

PARALLEL CAREER GOALS

GOAL ONE: FINANCE DIRECTOR	GOAL TWO: MANAGING DIRECTOR
CREATE A CHRONOLOGICAL RESUMÉ Focus on financial achievements	**CREATE A FUNCTIONAL RESUMÉ** Focus on managerial achievements
CONTACT RECRUITMENT COMPANIES Identify specialized financial recruitment companies	**CONTACT RECRUITMENT COMPANIES** Identify companies appointing senior staff
MONITOR RECRUITMENT ADVERTISEMENTS	**MONITOR RECRUITMENT ADVERTISEMENTS**
NETWORKING Conduct discreet research among fellow financial professionals	

TARGETING THE READER

Whatever strategy you choose to employ or route you take, an important consideration is the words you use – we all respond positively to people who "speak our language." Each audience has its own needs and priorities, so the content of your application needs to feed readers what they want to know. For example, try to employ specific phrases used in job advertisements, highlighting how you fit those requirements. With every job application, keep your targeted reader in mind and create both your resume and cover letter with their needs in mind.

13 Avoid filling your resumé with specialized terms.

14 Make sure that you appear flexible to a potential employer.

15 Carefully consider temporary roles – they may get you the job you want.

DO'S AND DON'TS

✔ Do be selective about to whom you send your resume.

✔ Do tell the reader what you want to do.

✔ Do ask the reader to respond.

✗ Don't send a resumé without a letter.

✗ Don't dismiss leads and openings too quickly.

✗ Don't expect a recruiter to give you career advice.

BEING FLEXIBLE

It is not just through applying for permanent jobs that you might join a new employer. Increasingly, many people join an organization through taking on consultancy assignments or filling a temporary role. For all employers, flexibility is a key word, so more temps, contractors, and consultants are employed than ever before. The same methods can be used as for finding permanent employment, but your proposition will need to be different.

You must also identify and target the correct person in either the employer or the recruitment company. With employers, contacting relevant line managers may be more productive than going through the personnel department.

THINKING AHEAD ▶
By being flexible in your approach, you will create many new opportunities for yourself.

TARGETING YOUR RESUMÉ

In order to make your resumé as effective as possible, it helps to understand how it will be used by an employer or recruiter. Keep in mind that an employer will be looking beyond your skills and qualifications to ascertain if you will fit into their organizations' culture.

16 Remember, recruiters are working for employers.

WINNING THE READER

Unless you are very lucky, or possess scarce skills that are in demand, your resumé will be one of many to land on the reader's desk. Among recruiters, it is a source of continuing debate whether their primary aim is to select candidates for their positive attributes, or reject them by identifying reasons for their unsuitability for the job. In preparing your resumé and covering letter, count on the reader doing both. It can be for very trivial reasons that applications are rejected at the paper-sifting stage; the secret is to plan for this and to try to get inside the mind of the reader.

MAKING YOUR RESUMÉ SCANNER-FRIENDLY

Your resumé may not be read by human eyes. Some larger employers and recruitment companies will scan your resumé into recruitment systems. Their software then identifies key words and phrases in your resumé and matches these with the requirements of a role. These systems may be used whether you submit a hard copy or email a text file. In order to make your resumé scanner-friendly, first make a list of the key words and phrases that cover both your skills and experience, and then weave them into your resumé. Second, ensure that the layout is clear and has no unusual typefaces.

17 Keep copies of any applications you email.

18 Avoid companies you know have bad employment records.

MAKING THE ▶ RIGHT MOVE

As this case illustrates, the working environment of an organization is as important as the job itself. Be honest with yourself about the type of company culture that you will find challenging and enjoyable.

CASE STUDY

After gaining her English degree, Laura worked in a small publishing house for three years, where she was promoted twice. Shortly after her 25th birthday, she joined a larger international publisher where she hoped to gain broader experience and work overseas. Everyone congratulated her on making a good career move: bigger job, more money, larger company, more opportunity. However, she left after only nine months. The job was a good one, that she did well, but the greater formality of the company, the layers of management, the memo writing, and lack of social life with any of her colleagues was not her style. When she applied for her next job, this time with a smaller company, she was careful to match the probable company culture with her own desire to work in a smaller, less structured, and more friendly environment.

LOOKING FOR A MATCH

Employers and recruiters are trying to identify a match between you, the job you are applying for, and the organization's culture. This is the basis of all good employment relationships, and as a result you are more likely to become a committed and motivated employee. When screening your resume, the reader will not only be looking for evidence of your capability to do the job, but also trying to judge whether you are the sort of person who will fit in to the culture of the organization.

19 Think hard about the working environment that will suit you.

The style and behavior of the organization matches your own personality. You respond positively to the working environment

The requirements of the role match your skills and experience. You can do the job today and are positive about where it might lead in future

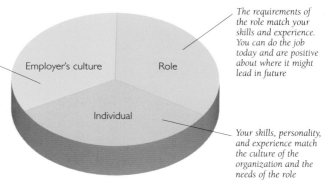

Employer's culture

Role

Individual

FINDING A ▶ MATCH

Aim to find a job match that balances the needs of your employer, your role, and you, the individual.

Your skills, personality, and experience match the culture of the organization and the needs of the role

UNDERSTANDING TRANSFERABLE SKILLS

Your qualifications and experience are only part of your personal assets. Your behavior as an individual is more important to employers than what you know, and they are more interested in what you can do in the future than what you have done in the past.

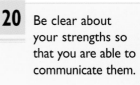

20 Be clear about your strengths so that you are able to communicate them.

QUESTIONS TO ASK YOURSELF

Q Which skills lie behind the work I enjoy doing?

Q Do I use skills in my personal life that people do not see at work?

Q Who can I ask to give me an objective opinion about my transferable skills?

Q Which skills do I want to develop and use again?

IDENTIFYING SKILLS

Transferable skills, core skills, soft skills, personal attributes, competences – these are all broad terms used to describe the same thing: the underlying aspects of you as an individual that indicate how suited you will be to a particular role. They relate to your behavior, personality, values, and motives, as well as to your skills and experience. By looking at the chart opposite, you will see that you possess some of the skills listed. But you will also have skills that are not so readily identified, and it is important that your resumé is able to pinpoint these.

LOOKING FOR EVIDENCE

A resumé is a highly subjective document. It is based on your own assessment of yourself. However, the more objective your resumé can become, the more powerful it will be. Anyone can claim to possess excellence in all the transferable skills listed opposite, but they will not be believed. However, if you can demonstrate evidence of possessing transferable skills through your past achievements, you will appear credible in your claim. Remember to always back up your claims with the hard evidence of results.

21 Demonstrate your skills through events in your past.

22 Add your non-work skills to your resumé.

Transferable Skills

Managerial Qualities

- **Leadership**
  Motivates others to reach team goals.
- **Planning and Organizing**
  Organizes and schedules events, activities, and resources. Monitors timescales and plans.
- **Quality Orientation**
  Ensures quality standards are met.
- **Persuasiveness**
  Influences and convinces others leading to acceptance, agreement, or behavior change.

Professional Qualities

- **Specialized Knowledge**
  Understands technical or professional aspects of work, and updates knowledge.
- **Problem-Solving and Analysis**
  Analyzes issues and makes systematic and rational judgments based on information.
- **Oral Communication**
  Speaks fluently to individuals and groups.
- **Written Communication**
  Writes in a clear, concise, relevant manner.

Entrepreneurial Qualities

- **Commercial Awareness**
  Understands commercial principles. Views issues in terms of costs, profits, and added value.
- **Creativity and Innovation**
  Creates new and imaginative approaches, and questions traditional assumptions.
- **Action Orientation**
  Makes decisions, takes initiative, and originates action.
- **Strategic Thinking**
  Demonstrates a broad-based view of issues.

Personal Qualities

- **Interpersonal Sensitivity**
  Interacts with others in a sensitive and effective way.
- **Flexibility**
  Adapts to changing demands and conditions.
- **Resilience**
  Maintains effective behavior in the face of setbacks or pressure.
- **Personal Motivation**
  Shows enthusiasm for goals and career commitment.

IDENTIFYING YOUR TRANSFERABLE SKILLS

The instructions that follow will help you to carry out a mini-audit of your career to identify your transferable skills. However, it is not enough to simply pinpoint your skills – you also need to think about how much you enjoy using them.

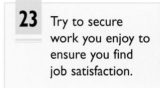

23 Try to secure work you enjoy to ensure you find job satisfaction.

THINGS TO DO

1. Write a brief outline of your career to date for quick and easy reference.

2. Keep all the notes you have made about your skills and objectives.

3. Keep ready to hand a copy of your present job description to refer to.

LISTING ACHIEVEMENTS

First, identify a minimum of ten achievements of which you are proud. They may come from your personal or work life – the balance will depend on your circumstances. Think creatively about what you might count as achievements – they are not just the obvious things. In your personal life, you may hold a position of responsibility that calls for the use of skills you do not normally use at work. You could also have had to deal with events that may not have been particularly enjoyable, but have nevertheless demonstrated capacities and talents you may not have realized you possess.

RECOGNIZING SKILLS

To identify your skills, break each achievement down into its component parts. Think about what each component part was and which skills you used. Using a chart such as the one opposite, score the frequency with which you used a transferable skill – you may be surprised by the results. (Refer to the list on p. 17 for detailed definitions.) Be aware of the skills you use in your personal life – some people find that their personal lives display a wider range of skills than they use at work.

24 Be honest when analyzing your skills – try not to be modest or arrogant.

DRAWING UP YOUR SKILLS CHART

List ten achievements

Identify the skills you used

Rate your enjoyment level and your wish to reuse skills

Discuss your assessment with a colleague

Review your results

SCORING AND CHECKING

Now rate on a scale of 1–5, where 1 is low and 5 is high, how much you enjoyed using each particular skill and then the degree to which you want to use it again. Being proficient at something and enjoying doing it are not always the same thing. Finally, take a reality check – this is not easy. Choose someone who knows you well and talk them through your analysis to come up with an overall reality rating for each skill.

25 Talk to friends and colleagues about what they identify as your strengths and weaknesses.

ASSESS RESULTS

Skills you can demonstrate and that you enjoy and want to use again are obvious priorities. Skills that you rate enjoyable and want to use again, but can only demonstrate limited evidence of, are clearly areas for career development. Keep the results of this mini-audit to help in preparing your resumé and cover letters – they are the key words, phrases, events, and ideas to include in all your applications.

FOCUSING ON ▶ STRENGTHS

A chart such as this one may seem time-consuming to produce, but it will prove an invaluable tool in your job search.

	Frequency	Enjoyment	Reuse	Reality
Managerial Qualities				
Leadership	3	4	4	3
Planning and Organizing	2	3	4	2
Quality Orientation				
Persuasiveness				
Professional Qualities				
Specialized Knowledge				
Problem-Solving and Analysis				
Oral Communication				
Written Communication				
Entrepreneurial Qualities				
Commercial Awareness				
Creativity and Innovation				
Action Orientation				
Strategic Thinking				
Personal Qualities				
Interpersonal Sensitivity				
Flexibility				
Resilience				
Personal Motivation				

Give a score of 1–5 for each of your skills in every category

Assess a number of skills relevant to your personal life

CREATING YOUR RESUMÉ

The content of your resumé needs to be prepared with meticulous attention to detail. Set aside plenty of time to write, edit, and design the layout of your resumé for maximum effect.

PREPARING THE CONTENT

Your resumé and letter are often the first contact you have with a prospective employer, and may receive just 30 seconds of their time on first reading. Ensure that your resumé contains the right information, in the right order, in a form that is easy to read.

26 Avoid using overly formal language in your resumé or cover letter.

27 Ensure that your resumé is concise and easy to read.

28 You have complete control over what to include in your resumé.

CREATING A GOOD FIRST IMPRESSION

Every part of your application must be an invitation to read more. A succinct and relevant cover letter will encourage the reader to turn to the resumé. A concise page will encourage the reader to look beyond your qualifications and current position. Remember, these initial, vital impressions have to achieve one thing: to ensure that your application is put on the "possible" pile. Decide whether a functional or chronological resumé is more appropriate for your application – the reader must know right away why you can do the job.

Use good-quality paper and a clear, pleasing layout	**Shows that you are businesslike and organized**
Write in an easily readable style, with good use of English	**Shows that you have good communication and literary skills**
Communicate complicated subjects simply and clearly	**Shows that you are a concise thinker**
Include relevant information with no spelling mistakes	**Shows that you have good attention to detail**
Select relevant information and career details	**Shows that you have good judgment**
Include appropriate qualifications and employment history	**Shows that you are qualified to do the job**

◀ **CONVEYING A MESSAGE**
The 30 seconds that an experienced recruiter may spend looking at your resumé will tell them much about you as a prospective candidate. Everything, from the type of information you include, through to the paper and envelopes you choose, says something about you.

DECIDING ON LENGTH

How long should your resumé be? The one-page summary is the general rule in the US, but two pages is a permissible exception. In one page you should be able to provide a convincing record of your recent achievements, outline your relevant experience and qualifications, and give the reader sufficient information to make the decision that you are worth seeing. If you are required to list technical skills or publications, then a separate page may be acceptable. Be rigorous about editing out anything that is not relevant.

RANKING INFORMATION

You are writing your resumé for the reader, not for yourself. It is down to you to judge the importance of different types of information through the reader's eyes; your educational achievements may be impressive, but if these are not a top priority to the reader, leave them until later. As the reader progresses through your resumé, there must be a clear and distinct ranking order that moves from essential information to additional information.

29 Be sure that your abilities are not obscured by too much detail.

DESCRIBING YOURSELF

You may use only 100 words to describe yourself in your resumé, but the impression these few words leave and the conclusions readers draw from them are vital. Plan this aspect with precision, as with every other aspect of preparing a resumé.

30 Put degree letters after your name only if they are really relevant.

31 Make sure that your voice-mail message is clear and businesslike in case potential employers call.

DEVELOPING A PERSONAL STYLE

It is not just what you say, it is the way that you say it. Too many job applicants resort to an old-fashioned, overly formal style of writing in their resumé construction and letter writing. In some cases, this even extends to writing the resumé in the third person. In everything you write, adopt a plain-speaking, jargon-free style that allows the content to shine through.

BEING YOURSELF

Your name is the first line of your resumé. But before you start, remember the one golden rule of resumé construction: you are creating a document of which you will be proud to say, "This is me." So, if you are Mike Bagshaw in your work life, be Mike Bagshaw on your resumé. Do not become Michael Bagshaw, or G. Michael Bagshaw, or Gordon MICHAEL Bagshaw, or G. M. Bagshaw, or Gordon M. Bagshaw, unless that is actually your "trading identity." If you have professional qualifications or accreditations, decide whether to include these after your name. The general rule is, if they are relevant to your application they should be included. However, if they are not relevant, or are purchased memberships, then they are best avoided altogether in your resumé.

QUESTIONS TO ASK YOURSELF

Q Reading through my resumé, does it sound like me?

Q Do I want to be contacted at work or will this jeopardize my current position?

Q Is my resumé written in plain English that a nonspecialist could understand?

Q Is there any personal information that is particularly relevant to my application?

Q Does my selection of personal information give an impression that I am happy with and can justify?

GIVING CONTACT INFORMATION

You must make it as easy as possible for interested readers to contact you. Clearly your full address is essential; although if you spend significant periods away, make this clear and offer an alternative means of contact. Include as many telephone contact points as you can – a work number, if you can take calls there, and a mobile number if you have one. Email is increasingly used, so include a personal email address if you have regular access to one.

32 Include your nationality if applying for jobs overseas.

▼ PROVIDING CONTACT INFORMATION

The contact information you give should be clear. An employer or recruiter will not want to try to get hold of you on several different numbers. Make sure you check for messages regularly.

Ensure your name is clear and easy to read

Include your ZIP code – it shows attention to detail

Neil Thomas
1060 West Addison
Chicago, Il 60613

Tel/Fax: (773) 555-1212
Mobile: (773) 555-1234
E-mail: Nthomas@brinter.com

Use your home rather than work email address

OWNING UP TO AGE

In the US, information about your age should not be included, but in the UK it is seen as a relevant piece of information. If your application is for a job overseas, it might be wise to include your age. The reader will guess at your age from other dates in your resume, so there is no point in leaving it out. The rule to follow is, if you believe your age is significant to your application, include it.

CULTURE BOX

Every country in the world has its own conventions about what is and is not included in a resume. The US has the strictest laws governing what an employer is entitled to know about you as an individual. In continental Europe it is more usual to include a photograph with an application, particularly in Germany and the Benelux countries. Detailed descriptions of schooling and higher education are also usually required in Europe. On occasions in Japan and the Far East, only graduates of certain universities may apply to particular employers.

33 Reveal only positive information about yourself in the resumé.

POINTS TO REMEMBER

- Too many time-consuming interests may suggest you have little time for work.
- Your interests may be open to negative interpretation.
- Employers will only be interested in your home life in as far as it has an impact on your working life.
- Employers will draw conclusions about the type of person you are from your interests.
- Any personal successes or achievements outside work should be highlighted.

INCLUDING RELEVANT PERSONAL INFORMATION

Conventions vary from country to country, but whether you are single, married, separated, or divorced, this is one aspect of your resumé that is hard to get right. Sometimes – for example, when the job involves travel – it may appear positive to be single. However, if the job requires someone who is settled and secure, a married person may seem more suitable. In fact, neither presumption is at all correct. If you choose to include your marital and family status, be aware of two things: first, ask yourself what conclusions someone screening your resumé might draw from your statements. Second, decide whether you believe it is relevant to the application you are making. If it is, and you choose to include it, it is best at the end.

34 Remember that you may be asked about anything and everything you have included in your resumé.

CASE STUDY

Terry and his wife lived in Seattle, but were brought up in the East and were eager to return after the birth of their two daughters. His family sent the classifieds from their local newspapers, and he started applying for jobs. Although a well-qualified engineer, Terry was getting nowhere with the jobs he applied for. A friend in human resources looked at his resumé and told him to

make one small change. Where he had put "married, 2 children" he should add "eager to relocate to home area." His friend explained that, faced with many suitable applicants, an employer may be put off by the prospect of a candidate whose family would have to resettle to a new area and meet the costs of relocation. In a 30-second read of his resumé, the Seattle address and "married, 2 children" were working against him.

◀ CLARIFYING INFORMATION
As with this case, make it clear, in both your resumé and cover letter, why your application should be taken seriously. If there are issues such as relocation or extensive traveling, reassure employers that you are happy about the prospect. Avoid putting yourself in the position of being rejected through a misunderstanding of your circumstances.

EMPHASIZING INTERESTS

What you do in your spare time can say a great deal about you. So you must be aware that in selecting which interests you include, you are painting a picture of yourself for the reader. Rock climbing or walking suggest you are active, while pursuits such as archaeology or reading indicate that you have an inquisitive mind. A penchant for DIY may show that you are practical, while painting or music suggests creativity. If you take part in charity work, the reader may infer that you are socially conscious, while youth work or chairing voluntary bodies may show your leadership potential. Sports can suggest either a competitive individual, or a team player.

▲ COMPLETING THE PICTURE
Your interests give you an opportunity to tell an employer a little more about yourself than simply your work achievements to date. Try to make the information relevant and emphasize the useful skills that you have mastered in pursuit of your interests.

35 Try to sound as objective as possible.

36 Avoid the use of "I" – it is implied throughout.

BEING AWARE OF BIAS

All good recruitment is about discrimination – discrimination in favor of the more able candidate. However, you must also count on some of the readers of your resumé succumbing to less constructive bias. Like it or not, presumptions will be made from whatever personal information you include on your resumé. By combining elements of that information, it is possible for readers to draw unethical and inappropriate conclusions about gender, race, and sexual orientation. So be careful not to provide too much information that could be negatively misconstrued.

SUMMARIZING EDUCATION AND TRAINING

The achievements you gain through education and training represent both acquired knowledge and your ability to develop. Many employers spend a lot of money on training and are looking to see if you are a person they should invest in.

37 Highlight any training undertaken through your own initiative.

DESCRIBING EDUCATION

There is one simple guideline here. The more recent your education, the more complete the description needs to be. At age 23 your educational record will form an important part of your achievements, and will be of significant interest to an employer. However, at age 43 your employment history counts for far more. Your education is, for the most part, of only passing interest. For both educational attainment and professional qualifications, the guideline is that the more recent and more relevant they are to your application, the more complete the description and the earlier they should appear in your resumé. Less recent and less relevant qualifications should be left down or out. Your resumé is your first opportunity to highlight your achievements, so consider heading this section "Qualifications Gained" or "Educational Achievements," thereby introducing a positive vocabulary.

38 Leave out any exams or courses in which you have been unsuccessful.

▼ **KEEPING UP TO DATE**
There are many courses available that you can use to update your IT skills. Initiating your own training shows you are motivated.

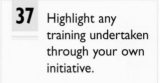

OUTLINING PERSONAL AND CAREER DEVELOPMENT

If you have a formal professional qualification, the details of this need to be included with your educational history. However, unless critical to a particular job application, details of other training do not generally merit an appearance. If using a second page, consider heading a section "professional and personal development." Under this you could include formal training as well as initiatives you have undertaken that do not carry a degree but are important to your career development.

▼ TRAINING RECORD

If you have an impressive record of training courses, you should mention the topics and dates – but limit it to those that are recent and relevant.

39 List your academic achievements and career history to date in reverse chronological order.

DO'S AND DON'TS

✔ Do consider the relevance of your academic record to an employer.

✔ Do include any special citations in exams or courses, if relevant.

✔ Do regularly update your IT skills.

✔ Do make this part of your resumé positive.

✘ Don't include "purchased" qualifications.

✘ Don't include "weak" subjects, such as a foreign language.

✘ Don't include training that has no bearing on an application.

✘ Don't go into unnecessary detail.

AVOIDING OVERLOAD

Be careful not to let your skills and experience get lost in a resumé that contains much irrelevant information. Space in your resumé is precious, so the following can generally be omitted (unless specifically requested or particularly relevant to your application): health, driver's license details, social security number, nationality, passport number, place of birth, next of kin, names and ages of your children.

SELLING YOUR EXPERIENCE

*H*aving described yourself and your qualifications, you now have to convince an employer that you have the right experience and attitude. It is important that the language of this part of your resumé is positive, jargon-free, and concise.

40 Read your resumé to a friend when checking for clarity and fluency.

THINGS TO DO

1. Check each sentence carefully, word by word, and delete any unnecessary or irrelevant words.
2. Make a list of words appropriate to your job and skills.
3. Take time to find alternative words and phrases to avoid being repetitious.

USING THE RIGHT WORDS

Creating a positive first impression depends on your vocabulary and tone, as well as the facts that you are putting across. For the most part, your resumé looks at your career in retrospect, so you should use the past tense. However, when describing current challenges, the present tense sounds more active. Never use "I" and avoid "me" or "my" – they can appear boastful and over-confident when you are trying to make your resumé appear an objective appraisal of your abilities. Look at the list of action words opposite and focus your mind on the type of words that should appear in your resumé. Compile a list that is specific to you.

USING POSITIVE LANGUAGE

It is vital that you write your resumé and covering letters with confidence. There is no better way of displaying that confidence to prospective employers than by using positive language to describe positive situations. Here are some examples of how to improve phrases:

❝ *Met project timescale* ❞
becomes
❝ *Achieved project timescale* ❞

❝ *Responsible for repair program* ❞
becomes
❝ *Headed repair program* ❞

❝ *Implemented quality procedures* ❞
becomes
❝ *Drove quality program* ❞

❝ *Suggested product enhancements* ❞
becomes
❝ *Devised product improvements* ❞

41 Draw on all your experience in drafting your resumé, and then edit it down.

USING A CAREER SUMMARY

The reader of your resumé should be able to pick out your skills and achievements instantly – most experienced recruiters will not take much notice of a career summary. There are, however, two cases where a summary may be useful: first, if you are writing to an individual inexperienced in reading resumés. Second, a career summary may help in a functional resumé in which your employment history does not clearly show your skills.

KEEPING IT CRISP

Short sentences are read and understood. Longer sentences incorporating too many ideas will lose the reader. Resumés that are written entirely in prose are difficult to scan quickly, but resumés that are endless lists and bullet points can be boring and characterless. You need to strike a balance.

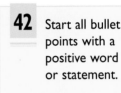

42 Start all bullet points with a positive word or statement.

INCORPORATING ACTION WORDS

USING INITIATIVE	SOLVING PROBLEMS	MANAGING SITUATIONS	ACHIEVING TARGETS
Bought	Advised	Appointed	Accomplished
Built	Analyzed	Appraised	Achieved
Created	Combined	Approved	Completed
Designed	Cut	Controlled	Conducted
Engineered	Examined	Developed	Delivered
Forecast	Identified	Directed	Demonstrated
Formed	Investigated	Drove	Exceeded
Generated	Reduced	Employed	Improved
Improvised	Reorganized	Guided	Increased
Initiated	Resolved	Headed	Obtained
Instigated	Revised	Inspired	Produced
Launched	Solved	Led	Promoted
Originated	Streamlined	Managed	Secured
Pioneered	Trimmed	Ran	Selected

DESCRIBING YOUR EXPERIENCE

A straightforward description of what you have done and who you did it for is not enough. The reader must be able to see your record of achievements, and so appreciate what you will be able to do in the future for their organization.

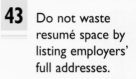

43 Do not waste resumé space by listing employers' full addresses.

ACHIEVEMENTS AND RESPONSIBILITIES

The most common complaint about many resumés is that they are no more than a series of job descriptions. What an employer needs to know is how well you did what you did. Your present job description may be a useful place to start, but it was prepared for another purpose. Your resumé needs to get you another job, and what you say about your responsibilities and achievements is critical.

POINTS TO REMEMBER

● An employer is looking for ability even more than experience – it points to the future.

● Specialized terms are only appropriate if you are sure the reader will understand them.

● The culture and ethos of your present organization may be of interest to a future employer.

44 Avoid exaggerating results, however important they are.

▼ **SHOWING OUTCOMES**
An event is of no significance without an outcome. Between the event and the outcome, add some quantifying detail.

DEFINING SUCCESS

All successes on your resumé must have features that are quantified and supported by outcomes. For example, "Led team of software developers" could be quantified to: "Led a team of 6 software developers on a $2m, 12-month project." There must also be an outcome – "Led a team of 6 software developers on a $2m, 12-month project. Achieved target timescale. Project gave 30 per-cent productivity gains for program users."

Event → **Quantify** → **Outcome**

DETAILING EMPLOYERS

You cannot assume that the reader will be familiar with the employers on your resumé. Even if you work for a well-known company, the department you work or worked for will not be known in detail. You need to briefly describe the core activity of the employer and put some detail to it. This could include sales turnover, number of employees, profits – whatever relates most to your line of work. You may also hint at the "corporate health" of the organization at that time; was it thriving or undergoing a period of major change? This will help the reader put your experience in context.

◀ DESCRIBING JOBS
Two people with similar job descriptions may have very different work experiences. Employers like to know in which type of environment you are used to working.

EXECUTIVE OFFICE

OPEN-PLAN OFFICE ENVIRONMENT

45 Be confident and businesslike when describing your achievements.

46 Use numerals – they are quicker and easier to read than words.

USING JOB TITLES

Both the content of your job and the job title itself will need some clarification. The meaning of a job title may vary from one organization to another, so use a generic job title if you can. It is better to write "Manager – International assignments" than "International assignment manager." You will also need to summarize your responsibilities. One way of doing this is through a short, one- or two-sentence précis, or use a heading such as "accountabilities" or "responsibilities." Finally, avoid using too much space to state the obvious, but make sure you include any interesting, unique, or unusual aspects of your role.

QUOTING DATES

Readers do not like gaps, and yet many people's careers will have them. You need to demonstrate a record of progression, but you do not need to account for every month of your life, so stick to years when giving employment dates. If you have had more than one job with the same employer, use one overall heading for the employer, with starting and finishing dates, and then treat each role as a sub-heading – giving dates for each. If you are currently out of work, do not suggest you are, as your employment status will become apparent.

48 Ensure your resumé spans your whole career, though you do not always need to go into details.

USING BULLET POINTS AND NUMBERS

A bullet point or number is an invitation to the eye to "read this," and it helps the reader to scan your resumé.

- Start each bullet point with a positive action word.
- Avoid starting a bullet point with a qualification, such as, "As part of project team provided..." or a passive statement, like, "Participated as a member..."
- Where the nature of your experience makes it appropriate to do so, group your achievements under numbered paragraphs, each of which has a number of specific features.

47 Put all of the most important information on the left of your resumé.

QUESTIONS TO ASK YOURSELF

Q Have I covered all periods of employment?

Q Have I included too many irrelevant details about earlier jobs?

Q Have I been consistent in my use of headings and bulleted points?

Q Is the language of my resumé positive without sounding overbearing?

GROUPING JOBS TOGETHER

At some points in your life, you may have worked in quick succession in a number of jobs. If these were with the same employer, try to group these together under generic headings and emphasize the range of experience gained. However, it must be clear to the reader that the high number of roles does not indicate that you were moved around or could not settle in any particular post. If the jobs were with different employers, were they permanent roles or was it a series of temporary engagements? Too much movement in the recent past can send a negative message.

DESCRIBING TEMPORARY JOBS

Many people use temporary employment as a means to an end at different stages of their careers. At the outset, this may have been to fund a university education, or gain work experience. Later, it could be a vehicle for returning to work, or as a stopgap between permanent jobs. Do not feel obliged to describe each of these assignments in detail. A prospective employer will be more interested in the initiative and commitment you have shown in taking temporary work. It may also give you the opportunity to highlight a diverse range of experiences gained through a variety of different assignments and working environments.

▼ RANKING INFORMATION

A prospective employer giving your resumé a 30-second scan needs to be able to see who you worked for, what your job title was, and what you achieved.

Employer's or company's name (and worked dates)

Your job title
Write a brief description of the employer's business, and include how many staff the company employs, how many staff worked under you or whether you were part of a team, and an estimate of annual turnover if applicable. Next, summarize your responsibilities in two or three short sentences. Then comes the most important part:

Achievements
● Make a bullet-pointed list of some of your key achievements.
● Demonstrate your potential value to prospective employer.
● Include anything that you think is relevant to your application.
● Also include nonwork achievements if you think they will help.

Items highlighted by bullet points will be picked out by an employer scanning your resumé

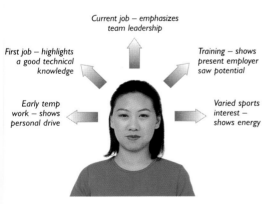

Current job – emphasizes team leadership

First job – highlights a good technical knowledge

Training – shows present employer saw potential

Early temp work – shows personal drive

Varied sports interest – shows energy

▲ BEING SELECTIVE
You can demonstrate to a potential employer that you have good judgment by the information you include in your resume. You need to select relevant experiences and then go on to highlight the reasons for their relevance to your application.

DESCRIBING PREVIOUS WORK

As you progress through your resumé, the descriptions of previous employment should become shorter. Only relatively recent jobs require a full description of your achievements and responsibilities. While you may be very proud of what you achieved in a job ten or more years ago, this is unlikely to be of interest to the reader. Indeed, if your early employment is irrelevant to your current application, do not attempt to explain it at all; give only dates and the name of the employer.

DECIDING ON LOOK

There is no right way to lay out your resumé, but there are plenty of things to avoid. Visual layout is probably the most subjective aspect of your preparation, but the objective is clear – to ensure your resumé is user-friendly and easy for the reader to scan.

49 Look at other people's resumés for layout and presentation ideas.

SELECTING A TYPEFACE

Keep it simple – you will not score any points for using fancy typefaces. What is more, if you email your resumé, you cannot guarantee the recipient's PC will be set up for non-standard typefaces. If your resumé is to be electronically scanned, the simpler the typeface the better.

50 Consider creating a style of resumé suited to email.

STRUCTURING YOUR RESUMÉ'S LAYOUT

There are essentially three core elements to your resumé. Each element must be easily recognizable to the reader as a distinct section.

- Contact information that is important enough to appear on top.
- Relevant employment and educational history.
- Relevant personal/professional information.

Times Roman

A classic, elegant face gives an impression of maturity

Italic may be hard to scan *Times Roman Italic*

Times Roman Bold

Bold type is good for picking out headings and dates Helvetica

Helvetica light

Helvetica Italic

A sans serif face is extremely easy to read

▲ COMMON TYPEFACES

The choice of a typeface is subjective; and the only important criterion is that it is easy to read. If it is one of the commonly used faces, it will be more easily scanned electronically. Only use one typeface throughout your resumé. Even if you are applying for a job in a design-based field, do not let the design hide the message.

Large headings waste
space and are unnecessary

16pt maximum for headings

12pt for body text
10pt for body text

Avoid making the
main text too small

▲ SETTING LEVELS
Use different type sizes for different levels
of information. Make sure that you are
consistent and that headings of the same
importance are the same size.

CHOOSING THE TYPE SIZE

Using too large a point size will waste valuable space, too small and the text can appear dense and difficult to read. Your resumé is a business document, so follow the usual practices for such correspondence. As a guide, use 10–12 points for the body text and nothing over 16 points for headings. Restrained use of bold text and capital letters will also help the reader pick out key facts.

51 Avoid using colored type – it may look good but it does not scan, photocopy, or email well.

CHOOSING PAPER AND ENVELOPES

Use good-quality 8½ x 11 in (21.5 x 28 cm) paper, white or near white. When choosing paper, think about the state your resumé will be received in – too thin and it will look cheap, too thick and it will always be creased. If posting your resumé, fold it only once and use an appropriately sized envelope.

Remember your
resumé will be
seen and handled
by many people;
the quality of
the paper and
envelopes you use
is very important

USING TEMPLATES

Many word processing packages will include standard templates for resumés. These can take some of the hard work out of the task of resumé preparation, and so are worth considering. However, be careful that the system does not prompt you to include unnecessary information or waste too much space. And remember, standard packages are just that – standard and ordinary – yet your resumé needs to be both unique and extraordinary.

CUSTOMIZING ▶ TEMPLATES
Use a computer
template to help with
the layout, not
the content of
your resumé.

GETTING IT RIGHT

Your resumé is almost complete. Having spent so much time deciding on content and layout, now comes the quality control stage. It is important to check your resumé thoroughly for mistakes: get a friend to give it a final read.

52 Use spell-checkers, but be aware that they will not find all mistakes.

POINTS TO REMEMBER

- All information that is specifically requested should be included.
- Employers want to know how well you did what you did, not just what you did.
- If asked to include salary details, consider including any important perks and bonuses.
- Useful feedback given by friends, recruiters, employers, and colleagues should be acted on.
- Achievements and transferable skills are the key interest points in your resumé for an employer.

53 If asked for a photograph, send a good quality one.

54 Include references only if specifically asked to do so.

THINGS TO AVOID

- **Do not lie:**
  It is accepted that your resumé will be a positive statement of your career to date. However, there is a clear line between favorable presentation and blatant misrepresentation. Do not claim you have attained qualifications you have not, attended courses you have not, or worked in roles you have not. If these are uncovered, your employer would be entitled to cancel your employment contract, since you misled them.

- **Do not include salary details:**
  As with most good brochures, the price list should be published separately. At this stage, the reader is assessing your suitability, so your remuneration is not relevant. However, you may be asked to provide current salary details, and/or a record of salary progression. This should be done in the cover letter.

- **Do not attach a photograph:**
  By preparing your resumé, you have carefully constructed a document that leads the reader to form a positive and objective opinion of you. The inclusion of a photograph may tempt a recruiter to make subjective decisions based on your appearance. However, the fashion or hospitality industries may request photographs, in which case you should include one.

GETTING A SECOND OPINION

Choosing someone to read your resumé is not easy, so it makes sense to ask someone who understands the work you do. More often than not, people are too diffident in what they write about themselves, so you may be encouraged to be more positive. Listen to the responses you get and decide what changes will improve your resumé.

55 If requested, include salary details in the covering letter.

Interviewee responds confidently to questions

Interviewer refers frequently to resumé

▲ APPEARING CONFIDENT

It is essential that you can expand on and justify everything in your resumé. Approach an interview with the same positive attitude you have brought to your resumé and letter writing.

DO'S AND DON'TS

☑ Do check punctuation, spelling, and tenses.

☑ Do use positive action words in both letters and resumés.

☑ Do adjust your resumé to different situations.

☒ Don't undersell yourself.

☒ Don't forget the importance of first impressions.

☒ Don't include references – they will be requested later.

PREPARING FOR INTERVIEWS

When your resumé has done its job and you are called for an interview with an employer or a recruiter, it is your resumé that will probably set the agenda for that meeting. Often the recruiters will know nothing more about you than is contained in your resumé. It is at this point that the quality of your resumé will show and any inconsistencies, flaws, or misunderstandings will come to light. Be prepared for any awkward questions you think may be raised and think about the answers you will give so that you can reinforce the positive impression given by your resumé.

56 Read your resumé again before going to an interview.

PUTTING YOUR RESUMÉ TOGETHER

The example resumés in this chapter show how different styles are appropriate at different times. Understanding these styles will enable you to produce the most effective resumé.

ADAPTING YOUR RESUMÉ

Your resumé is a living document – in fact, not just one document but many. Your life never stands still, so neither should your resumé. Just as different people see different sides of you at different times, your resumé should change according to the situation.

57 Be prepared to edit, re-edit, and revise your resumé many times.

QUESTIONS TO ASK YOURSELF

Q Am I looking for a change of direction in my career?

Q Have I made a list of my transferable skills and career objectives that I can refer to?

Q Do I understand the difference between a functional and chronological style of resumé, and when to use each one?

Q Do my skills and experience match the jobs that I am applying for?

CHOOSING YOUR RESUMÉ

Too many people write their first resumé and then spend the rest of their career modifying the same document. But at different times of your life you will need different resumés. At some points in your career you will be selling your potential, at others, your employment history. However, it will always be your transferable skills that ultimately win you the job. Look at each of the example resumés in this chapter to see if there are elements that are relevant to you. Remember, whatever skills you are seeking to communicate in your resumé must also be supported by evidence of their use.

BEING AWARE ▶

As this case illustrates, the one overriding factor that influences the content and structure of your resumé is the job you are applying for. It is the person who is going to read your resumé, and what it is they are looking for, that should dictate how you put your resumé together.

CASE STUDY

Steve had worked for seven years in an advertising agency, rising to the position of group leader. However, he decided that the pressure of constant deadlines and frequent late nights were increasingly eating into his quality of life. In applying for jobs outside advertising, he at first used a conventional chronological resumé, but was advised that, for an employer outside the advertising sector, the job titles and companies he had worked for offered little insight to his abilities. After auditing his career, he identified his transferable skills and used a functional resumé, focusing on his skills in task management, training, team leadership, and attention to detail. Almost immediately, his conversion rate of applications sent to calls for interview improved. He now works in a team leadership role in the financial services industry.

TAILORING YOUR RESUMÉ

No two employers and no two jobs are identical, so no one leaves one job to fulfill exactly the same role for another employer. It therefore follows that in your job search one resumé will not fit all situations. Whether it is a matter of slightly modifying your resumé for a specific job application, or writing a completely new resumé, you should change your approach to meet the needs of each situation. This is particularly true if you are applying for jobs outside your own employment sector – here you are selling your potential to do well in a particular job, rather than selling your history of having done well in other jobs. You must also be prepared to skillfully tailor your resumé for a particular application in order to highlight the precise skills and range of experience you know an employer is looking for.

59 Make sure that, whatever job you are applying for, it is your skills and achievements that stand out.

58 Remember, an employer wants to see your potential.

THINGS TO DO

1. Read all relevant job advertisements.

2. Pick out the relevant skills and experience that each job application requires.

3. Consider connecting to email and the Internet if you think they will help.

4. Review your career objectives regularly, and carefully adapt them.

5. Ask a friend to read and comment on your draft resumé.

APPLYING FOR YOUR FIRST JOB

*A*t this stage, your resumé needs to show
your potential – that you are somebody
worth investing in. Employers may respond to
your resumé by sending you an application
form. Approach this as you have your resumé,
focusing on your achievements and skills.

60 Be creative in your approach to your resumé, but follow the basic rules.

FIRST JOB: FUNCTIONAL RESUMÉ

Start with a career objective if decided

↓

Include full details of your educational record

↓

Summarize your relevant achievements

↓

Describe any relevant work experience and skills

61 Remember, employers look for enthusiasm and motivation.

ORDERING INFORMATION

When looking for your first job, the best format for your resumé is the functional one. You need to list full details of your education – these will be your main achievements to date. Think hard about your other accomplishments – you will need to identify them from your academic, working, and personal life. They will then need to be described in a way that will make them appealing to an employer. If you know your career objective, include this first. Also include details of any work experience. If you have other skills, such as IT, round these up in a section entitled "Business Skills."

DO'S AND DON'TS

✔ Do identify key achievements that are relevant to your application.

✔ Do include details of education courses and examination results.

✔ Do include a relevant career objective.

✘ Don't include unnecessary details about temporary jobs.

✘ Don't be unrealistic in your aims.

✘ Don't waste space – it is perfectly acceptable for your resumé to fit on to one page.

STRESSING POTENTIAL ▼

A first resumé needs to list all academic achievements but, unless they are exceptional, your resumé will not stand out. To make your document distinctive, you need to concentrate on your skills and experience beyond your education.

62 If you are exploring more than one career path, create more than one resumé.

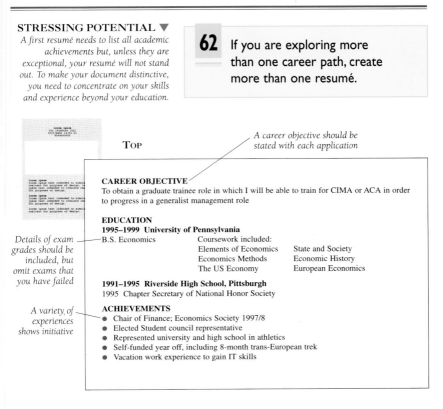

TOP

A career objective should be stated with each application

CAREER OBJECTIVE
To obtain a graduate trainee role in which I will be able to train for CIMA or ACA in order to progress in a generalist management role

EDUCATION
1995–1999 University of Pennsylvania

Details of exam grades should be included, but omit exams that you have failed

B.S. Economics

Coursework included:
Elements of Economics
Economics Methods
The US Economy

State and Society
Economic History
European Economics

1991–1995 Riverside High School, Pittsburgh
1995 Chapter Secretary of National Honor Society

A variety of experiences shows initiative

ACHIEVEMENTS
- Chair of Finance; Economics Society 1997/8
- Elected Student council representative
- Represented university and high school in athletics
- Self-funded year off, including 8-month trans-European trek
- Vacation work experience to gain IT skills

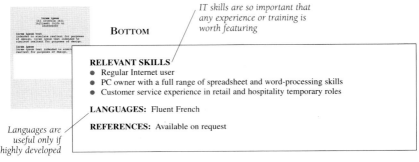

BOTTOM

IT skills are so important that any experience or training is worth featuring

RELEVANT SKILLS
- Regular Internet user
- PC owner with a full range of spreadsheet and word-processing skills
- Customer service experience in retail and hospitality temporary roles

LANGUAGES: Fluent French

REFERENCES: Available on request

Languages are useful only if highly developed

MAKING YOUR FIRST CAREER CHANGE

The work experience you have gained in your first job should equip you with the confidence to make a positive career move. You are also more likely to have a clear idea of what you want from your career and your next job.

63 Aim high, but be realistic about what your next move should be.

FIRST CAREER CHANGE: CHRONOLOGICAL RESUMÉ

Start with a brief summary of your educational record

⬇

Describe your current job, highlighting your achievements

⬇

Summarize other employment and include skills

⬇

Finish with other relevant personal information

64 Always appear positive about your work experiences.

ORDERING INFORMATION

Use the chronological format to produce the strongest resumé if your career move is within the same field. Your education is still recent enough to be of critical interest to an employer, so begin with a brief account. It is important to assess exactly what you have learned from your work experience and to emphasize your achievements – this is now the core of your resumé. Your career objectives will not appear on your resumé, but it is worth spending time clarifying what they are.

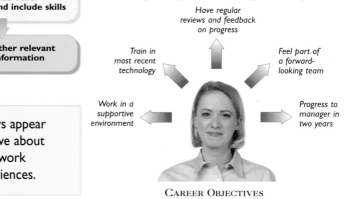

Have regular reviews and feedback on progress

Train in most recent technology

Feel part of a forward-looking team

Work in a supportive environment

Progress to manager in two years

CAREER OBJECTIVES

▼ PRIORITIZING INFORMATION

The emphasis of your resumé has moved from your personal life achievements to your career achievements, although any relevant personal accomplishments still deserve a mention.

TOP

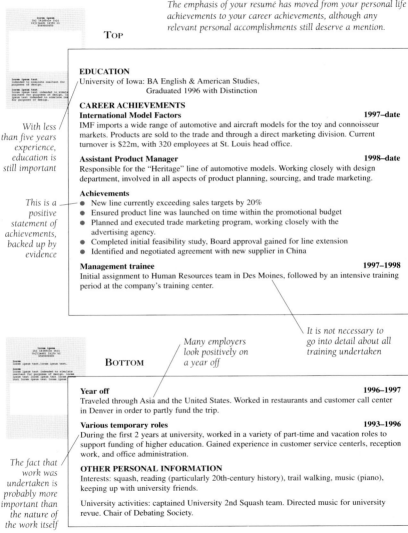

EDUCATION

University of Iowa: BA English & American Studies,
Graduated 1996 with Distinction

With less than five years experience, education is still important

CAREER ACHIEVEMENTS

International Model Factors   **1997–date**

IMF imports a wide range of automotive and aircraft models for the toy and connoisseur markets. Products are sold to the trade and through a direct marketing division. Current turnover is $22m, with 320 employees at St. Louis head office.

Assistant Product Manager   **1998–date**

Responsible for the "Heritage" line of automotive models. Working closely with design department, involved in all aspects of product planning, sourcing, and trade marketing.

Achievements

This is a positive statement of achievements, backed up by evidence

- New line currently exceeding sales targets by 20%
- Ensured product line was launched on time within the promotional budget
- Planned and executed trade marketing program, working closely with the advertising agency.
- Completed initial feasibility study, Board approval gained for line extension
- Identified and negotiated agreement with new supplier in China

Management trainee   **1997–1998**

Initial assignment to Human Resources team in Des Moines, followed by an intensive training period at the company's training center.

It is not necessary to go into detail about all training undertaken

Many employers look positively on a year off

BOTTOM

Year off   **1996–1997**

Traveled through Asia and the United States. Worked in restaurants and customer call center in Denver in order to partly fund the trip.

Various temporary roles   **1993–1996**

During the first 2 years at university, worked in a variety of part-time and vacation roles to support funding of higher education. Gained experience in customer service centerls, reception work, and office administration.

The fact that work was undertaken is probably more important than the nature of the work itself

OTHER PERSONAL INFORMATION

Interests: squash, reading (particularly 20th-century history), trail walking, music (piano), keeping up with university friends.

University activities: captained University 2nd Squash team. Directed music for university revue. Chair of Debating Society.

CHANGING JOBS MID-CAREER

With at least ten years' experience behind you, your resumé has become your most important career document. It must reflect all the commitment you have made to your career and the achievements that now make you marketable.

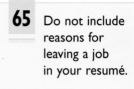

65 Do not include reasons for leaving a job in your resumé.

MID-CAREER CHANGE: CHRONOLOGICAL RESUMÉ

Start with a detailed account of your current employment

Give a full list of all your significant achievements

Summarize your previous employment and roles

End with any other relevant personal or educational details

66 Make the most of all the professional and social contacts you have.

ORDERING INFORMATION

Unless you are considering a complete change of career, the chronological form of resumé is probably the preferred format. An accurate description of past and current responsibilities together with your record of achievements is critical – what you do now, and have done in the past, are the key elements of your document. Details of your education are less important – relevant education and qualifications should appear, but after your employment record. Remember the "more relevant, more recent" rule. Summarize earlier employment, and spell out details of professional development in full.

QUESTIONS TO ASK YOURSELF

Q What methods should I use to find a new job?

Q Who can I talk to off-the-record about my next move?

Q Am I clear about my priorities, both career and lifestyle?

Q When would be the best time to start applying for a job?

Q How soon do I want to leave my current employment?

Q Am I prepared to relocate – in this country or abroad?

SHOWING RESULTS ▼

At this level a future employer wants proof of your effectiveness – a certain amount of statistics help to make your resumé appear more businesslike.

67 Use the past tense in your resumé – for example, "managed" not "managing" – it will read better.

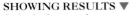

TOP

Some explanation of an employer's activites is helpful, and figures give substance

CAREER SUMMARY
Electron Group International (EGI)   **1996–present**
Human Resources Director, Europe.
EGI designs and manufactures semiconductor processing and measurement equipment. The European Division has 5 principal development/manufacturing sites (UK, France, Germany, Italy, Ireland) and a further 8 sales/service locations. 1999 European sales Euro364m, European employees 3,800.

A very brief job description is all that is needed

Responsible at Divisional Board level for all HR activities. Pan-European team of 65 HR professionals based in 9 locations.

Achievements

Although brief, these points cover a range of activities

- Established HR team from scratch in 4 locations
- Negotiated pan-European pay & benefits review
- Recruited 22 senior managers across all management functions
- Restructured HR team and functional responsibilities
- Led Divisional project team investigating new manufacturing location
- Resolved EU training grant dispute

BOTTOM

This is included to account for a time which would otherwise look like an unexplained gap

Various temporary roles   **1977–1979**
Prior to taking an overseas graduate traineeship, worked in a variety of temporary roles in the US and Europe.

EDUCATION & PROFESSIONAL QUALIFICATIONS

Relevant professional qualifications head the list

Fellow of Institute of Personnel Development (FIPD)		1989
University of Oregon: BS (Hons) Engineering		1977

PROFESSIONAL DEVELOPMENT

HR leadership short course	INSEAD	1997
Assessment Center Technology	Roffey Park	1991
Counseling skills at work	CEPEC	1989
Accredited to use aptitude & psychometric materials	Saville Worth	1985

This is useful as there may be a delay before an interview takes place

PERSONAL INFORMATION
Languages: German – fluent, Italian – business level

———————— Resumé compiled 9/18/99, all information correct at this date

LOOKING FOR A CHANGE OF DIRECTION

There was a time when a job was for life. This is no longer the case. You may be changing your career direction for all kinds of reasons. Whatever it is, you need to present your experience in a way that is attractive to those outside your sector.

68 See a new start as an opportunity to make the most of skills you enjoy.

CHANGE OF DIRECTION: FUNCTIONAL RESUMÉ

Include your career objective if you have one

↓

Start by highlighting your transferable skills

↓

Give a summary of your relevant employment history

↓

List relevant and recent education and courses

BRANCHING OUT ▼
Moving into a new field can be difficult. Be clear in your own mind of your worth to an employer.

ORDERING INFORMATION

Too many people seeking a change of career direction will use a chronological resumé format. This means that the potential employer must try to distill from a range of previous experience (which at first glance is not apparently relevant) the skills in which they may be interested. Much better that you use a functional resumé format that highlights your skills and supports these with your employment history. It is therefore critical that you have audited your career and identified your core skills. Be clear that those skills you are emphasizing will be attractive to an employer. If you have decided on a clear career objective, consider including it.

69 Highlight different core skills, depending on the nature of your application.

Identify your core skills → **State your career objectives** → **Tell an employer what you can do**

SOUNDING POSITIVE ▼

Emphasize your key skills – your actual career history can be dealt with quite briefly. Ensure that your cover letter sounds positive about your previous work experiences and eager for new challenges.

70 Make sure that you are seen as making a career change for all the right reasons.

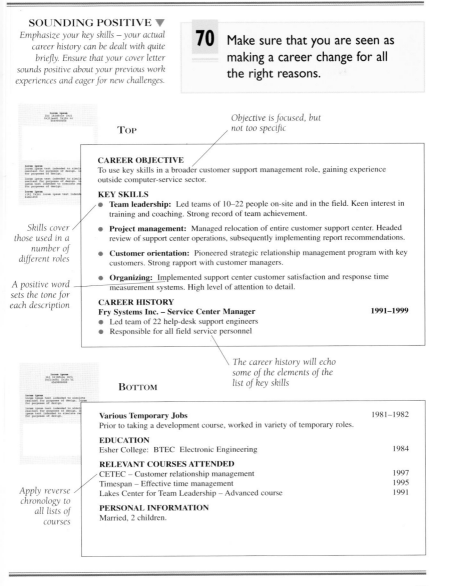

TOP

Objective is focused, but not too specific

CAREER OBJECTIVE
To use key skills in a broader customer support management role, gaining experience outside computer-service sector.

KEY SKILLS

- **Team leadership:** Led teams of 10–22 people on-site and in the field. Keen interest in training and coaching. Strong record of team achievement.

- **Project management:** Managed relocation of entire customer support center. Headed review of support center operations, subsequently implementing report recommendations.

- **Customer orientation:** Pioneered strategic relationship management program with key customers. Strong rapport with customer managers.

- **Organizing:** Implemented support center customer satisfaction and response time measurement systems. High level of attention to detail.

CAREER HISTORY
Fry Systems Inc. – Service Center Manager   **1991–1999**
- Led team of 22 help-desk support engineers
- Responsible for all field service personnel

Skills cover those used in a number of different roles

A positive word sets the tone for each description

The career history will echo some of the elements of the list of key skills

BOTTOM

Various Temporary Jobs   1981–1982
Prior to taking a development course, worked in variety of temporary roles.

EDUCATION
Esher College: BTEC Electronic Engineering   1984

RELEVANT COURSES ATTENDED
CETEC – Customer relationship management   1997
Timespan – Effective time management   1995
Lakes Center for Team Leadership – Advanced course   1991

PERSONAL INFORMATION
Married, 2 children.

Apply reverse chronology to all lists of courses

RETURNING TO WORK

As when you were first looking for a job, your main aim now is to convince an employer that you are worth investing in. You must show what you achieved before your break, and that you are motivated and eager to brush up on any rusty skills.

71 Make a point of learning IT skills at every possible opportunity.

RETURNING TO WORK: FUNCTIONAL RESUMÉ

Start with a profile of your experience and goals

List the transferable skills acquired during your career

Give details of your education and qualifications

Finally, list your achievements and relevant experience

72 Only you can judge a job against your lifestyle criteria.

SETTING PARAMETERS ▶
Be clear about how your working life needs to fit in with your personal life. However, do not spell it out in an application; you could appear to be inflexible.

ORDERING INFORMATION

After a break from work, it is unlikely that a chronological resumé will serve your purposes – you need to use a functional resumé to emphasize your skills and achievements. A short profile of yourself will help an employer see your worth. The skills that caused you to be successful before you took your career break were your transferable skills, and are just as relevant now as they were then. What may be a little out of date is your knowledge – your knowledge of the sector or your learned skills, such as IT. An employer needs to see your record of achievement before your break, and be convinced of your motivation.

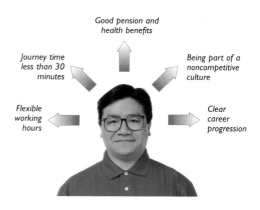

Good pension and health benefits

Journey time less than 30 minutes

Being part of a noncompetitive culture

Flexible working hours

Clear career progression

REASSESSING YOUR ▼
CAREER GOALS

Be selective about what you include in your resumé – account for your whole career and any breaks, but give details only if they will enhance your resumé.

73 Show that you are motivated by undertaking training while you are preparing to return to work.

TOP

This profile incorporates both a statement of career history and present objectives

PROFILE
Accomplished bilingual (French/English) Management Accountant with experience in the retail, distribution, and financial-services sectors, wishing to pursue a career in accounting and financial analysis.

KEY SKILLS

Your key skills will always be relevant

- Identifying management information needs and developing strategies to ensure user-friendly and precise reporting of financial performance.
- Ensuring accurate and timely reporting of financial performance at division and head office level. Experience of units with turnover of $2m to $100m.
- Designing and developing communication programs to help non-financial management understand management accounts.
- Selecting and recruiting finance-department staff at all levels.
- Managing and assessing training and development needs within finance departments.

There is no need for dates or employer specifics in this section

EDUCATION AND QUALIFICATIONS GAINED
CIMA: Gained 1991
Parkway College of Further Education, BTEC 1987.

Education is important if you are returning to work, since it shows concrete achievements

Keep details of previous employment brief and relevant, but still focus on achievements

BOTTOM

Barker Parts Distribution
Management Accountant 1988–1992
Appointed Divisional Management Accountant on qualification in 1991. Had joined as graduate trainee and was promoted 5 times in 4 years. Gained experience in France and Germany during 9-month assignment.

PERSONAL
Married, 2 children

Your interests may be relevant to an employer

Interests: Tennis, swimming, painting, photography.
References: Available on request.

USING YOUR RESUMÉ

The resumé you have spent so long creating now needs to do its job – to earn you interviews. In order for it to do that, you must send it with the right cover letter to the right people.

REPLYING TO JOB ADVERTISEMENTS

Job advertisements represent the most open recruitment marketplace. It is a highly competitive field, so your application needs to work hard for you. Careful preparation of a succinct cover letter is every bit as important as the resumé itself.

74 Thoroughly research every organization to which you apply.

Clearly mark any advertisements that look interesting

MATCHING YOURSELF UP

A job advertisement provides only very limited information about the employer and the role. Your challenge is to look behind the actual words, analyze the employer's needs, and match yourself to those criteria. The more precisely your skills can be linked to the job, the greater your chance of being shortlisted – a good guideline is that you should exceed 80 percent of the advertised requirements.

FOLLOWING INSTRUCTIONS

Read reply instructions carefully. One of the most common reasons for applications being rejected at the first screen is that the reply instructions have not been followed. You will usually be asked to quote a reference number, and may be asked for other information, such as salary progression, or expectations. Only rarely will advertisers come back to you to request information you have omitted – they will have plenty of other applicants who will have followed the instructions.

75 Help your resumé to stand out from the rest with a strong cover letter.

CULTURAL DIFFERENCES

In some countries a written, rather than typed, cover letter is expected. In France, in particular, handwritten letters are important as applicants' letters may be sent to a graphologist, who analyzes the handwriting to identify the characteristics of the writer.

DO'S AND DON'TS

✔ Do keep dated copies of all the job advertisements that you reply to.

✔ Do check if there is a closing date, and reply in plenty of time.

✔ Do write a relevant cover letter with every application.

✔ Do ensure your application passes the 30-second test.

✘ Don't get despondent if you are rejected – accept it and move on to the next application.

✘ Don't apply indiscriminately for jobs; each application you make needs to be focused.

✘ Don't ignore reply instructions.

✘ Don't omit specifically requested information.

PASSING THE FIRST SCREEN

You know that your application may not get more than a 30-second look the first time around. Check that you have done the following to ensure it passes that 30-second test and makes it to the next stage:
- You have followed reply instructions;
- Your overall presentation is good;
- Your written style is clear;
- You have been succinct;
- You have shown good attention to detail;
- You have displayed good judgment by selecting the right, relevant information.

76 Limit the number of applications you make each week.

77 Make your resumé as relevant as possible.

WRITING THE IDEAL COVER LETTER

In order to attract the most suitable applicants, job advertisements are very carefully worded. When replying to an advertisement, your cover letter needs to show you have understood the nature of the job being advertised. It must also summarize why your application should receive serious consideration. The letter opposite picks up on all important elements of the job advertisement below and feeds back key phrases. This letter should make it onto the "possible" pile.

78 Include a number of reasons why your application is a strong one.

The job title is the first clue to the nature of any job. The advertisement then clarifies how much experience the employer requires

MATCHING UP ▶

When replying to job advertisements, pick out the key skills and experience that are required for the position and demonstrate how you match them. In this example, the key opposite shows how the applicant gives evidence of his or her suitability for the job – and pays attention to getting the details right.

This company has big plans – it is expanding, so candidates need to be happy in a changing environment

There are a number of responsibilities listed – applicants need a range of skills

Experience in this sector is absolutely vital for this job

General Manager - Training Services ❶

Starting from scratch 5 years ago, Fountain Training has grown phenomenally and now employs 150 consultants working from 5 offices across the country ❺. We intend to continue our aggressive growth program and plan to open 2 offices overseas in the next 6 months.

We now wish to appoint a General Manger to head up 2 of our existing offices. You will be responsible for the smooth running of these operations ❺ while also ensuring we continue to grow market share. You will oversee the development of new training services ❼ and be responsible for the activities of the sales teams ❻.

You will need to have a close understanding of the training market ❼ ❽ and a record of success in a changing environment ❺. Excellent business awareness ❽ needs to be supported by a strong business drive and energy ❹ to produce results ❻. Above all you must be a good general manager and team player ❼ with the capacity to manage a growing number of profit centers ❿.

If you want to develop your career ❾ in the training industry, write to: ❷ Chris Williams, Human Resources Director, Fountain Training. Quote ref. no. 18/9DI ❶

79 Make sure you sign all your cover letters very clearly.

Key

❶ *Quotes reference number and job title at the start of the letter*

❷ *Uses first name, since he or she (never make assumptions) did in the advertisement*

❸ *Begins with an attention-grabbing opening that shows motivation*

❹ *Shows resourcefulness – this person has initiative and energy*

❺ *Highlights an understanding of the business and its changing demands*

❻ *Illustrates a real achievement in business development – a key skill for this job*

❼ *Underlines the candidate's experience as leader of a successful team*

❽ *Demonstrates real understanding of the advertiser's business*

❾ *Shows personal motivation and a belief in future career possibilities*

❿ *Demonstrates commitment and empathy: "I want to grow with you"*

Chris Williams
Human Resources Director
Fountain Training

❶ General Manager – Training Services: Your ref. 18/9DI

Dear Chris **❷**

As an experienced manager in the training industry, your advertisement in the Daily Informer intrigued me **❸**. Having read the advertisement closely and conducted a little background research through visiting your Web site **❹**, I believe I have a clear understanding of your needs. I hope you will agree my resumé warrants closer examination for the following reasons:

❺ I have worked in a high-growth environment for the past 3 years and so am fully aware of the demands this places on operational management.

❻ I am currently responsible for all sales development activities at SKH Associates, the team having exceeded sales targets for the past 2 years.

❼ I led the team, which gained industry accreditation 6 months ago.

❽ Coming from a background as a front-line trainer, I continue to maintain close links with our employer client base and training industry standards bodies.

The role of General Manger would be a natural career progression for me **❾**, and I believe that, with your commitment to continued growth, Fountain Training would be an ideal environment in which to develop my career over the longer term **❿**.

I would welcome the opportunity of discussing this opportunity further with you.

Yours sincerely

CONTACTING RECRUITMENT COMPANIES

It is employers who pay the recruitment companies' fees – they are not there to give you free advice and support, but to find the right candidate for a particular role. However, they are the gateway to many jobs, and you must know how to deal with them.

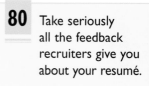

80 Take seriously all the feedback recruiters give you about your resumé.

81 Make a note of the recruitment applications you make and follow them up.

FINDING A CONTACT

If you plan to contact a recruitment company "cold" or speculatively, it is prudent to write to a named individual. In some firms this may simply be the person responsible for inputting resumés into databases. However, the best policy is to telephone to find the name of the person who deals with the job area, industry, and/or location in which you are most interested.

IDENTIFYING THE RIGHT RECRUITMENT COMPANY

TYPE OF COMPANY	SERVICE PROVIDED
SEARCH AND SELECTION Handles middle- to senior-management roles in general and specialized fields.	Usually conducts a specific search assignment for each vacancy, but will hold details of prospective candidates on file.
SPECIALIZED RECRUITMENT COMPANY Operates in most functional and specialized areas at all levels.	Holds databases of suitably qualified candidates and has a specialized knowledge of a particular industry or profession.
EMPLOYMENT AGENCY Handles vacancies up to first-line management or supervisory level.	Operates on a local basis at the less specialized end of recruitment, although some will have specialized divisions.

THINGS TO DO

1. Use business directories to find appropriate recruitment companies.

2. Use the Internet to find recruitment sites.

3. Scan classifieds for relevant recruitment agencies.

4. Follow up all unanswered applications.

DECIDING ON YOUR MESSAGE

When writing speculatively, you will be asking to be considered for assignments where your skills and experience are suitable, so be sure to make them clear. In the case of the specialized recruitment companies and employment agencies, your target is an exploratory meeting, where one of their consultants will be able to gain an in-depth appreciation of you. Search and selection firms will tend not to see candidates on a speculative basis, preferring to make appointments only when they are handling a relevant assignment.

GETTING FEEDBACK

If you are rejected at the first stage, you just have to accept that there were better qualified candidates. Occasionally, however, you may feel that you were so close to the specification that you would like some explanation from the recruitment company. Do not question their judgment – ask for constructive feedback about why they rejected you, and how you might better present your case in future.

Keep a note of contacts' names, making sure you have the right spelling

KEEPING RECORDS ▶
Your job search is likely to stretch over several months. Good record-keeping of contacts and follow-up communication will make the whole process less stressful.

82 Put the date at the bottom of all the resumés you send out.

FOLLOWING UP

If you have written speculatively to a recruitment company, it is reasonable to expect some sort of response. Ideally, this will be an invitation to meet, but it may just be an undertaking to hold your details on file. If you have heard nothing after about three months, consider contacting them again and sending a fresh copy of your resumé.

83 Write short, clear sentences in your letter and your resumé.

84 Type letters unless you are specifically asked to write them by hand.

COMPOSING A "COLD" OR SPECULATIVE LETTER

Put yourself in the position of the recruiter and remember that they may receive hundreds of speculative letters every week. Try opening your letter with a positive statement. In order to get the reader's attention it can be a good ploy to start with "you" or "your" – for example, "Your company has an impressive reputation in the recruitment of..." or, "You are one of a very few recruitment consultants..." The letter needs to describe the key aspects of your resumé succinctly and say why the consultant should be interested in you. You must finally make a clear proposition and leave the reader in no doubt of your career objective.

Hilary Rahman
Accountancy Selection Inc.

Addressing a named individual is very important

Dear Hilary

Your company enjoys an excellent reputation in the recruitment of accountants.

Flattery can be effective, but do not be too gushing – it may come across as insincere

Having built up 5 years' post-qualification experience, I now feel it is time to move on and seek my first financial controller role. My resumé is attached, and I hope you agree that I will make a strong candidate for the following reasons:

Bullet points pick out why this person is a strong candidate and summarize their career and present situation

● Qualified ACA
● 5 years' post-qualification experience
● 3 years spent in industry role
● Fully mobile, willing to relocate

Having already stated career goals, the letter ends with an invitation for the recruiter to reply

I hope you or your firm may be handling suitable assignments currently or in the near future. I would be very interested to meet with you and discuss any such opportunities.

Yours sincerely

▲ STATING YOUR AIMS
This is a straightforward letter, written in plain English. It states very clearly the strengths of the candidate, and exactly the sort of jobs he or she would like to be considered for.

85 Be confident about demonstrating your industry-specific knowledge.

Use of the correct name, and any title, immediately shows initiative

Letter begins by establishing present status and key achievements

Awkward questions about reasons for looking for a new job are pre-empted

Mr. A. Mitchell
Hayward Search Consultants

Dear Mr. Mitchell

As Production Director of March Plastics, I have over the past 5 years led a revolution in the manufacture of our core product: disposable cutlery. However, the next phase of this program is consolidation, and so the same level of challenge will not be present. I have therefore decided it is time to look for a move.

As you will see from my resumé, I have a wide range of manufacturing experience; and for the past 8 years have operated at Board level. I know from colleagues that you have handled similar positions, so I would like to be considered for any current or future assignments.

My desired salary package is $50,000 plus the usual executive benefits. I would prefer not to relocate; although, as I have commuted weekly for the past 3 years, I would like to be considered for any suitable role anywhere in the country.

I would be happy to meet with you or a colleague to discuss any suitable opportunities.

Yours sincerely

Seniority of the applicant is emphasized

Purpose of the letter is to sell, but the tone is not pushy

Location preference is given, but flexibility is stressed

Inclusion of current salary indicates desired salary level

This is the correct sign-off for a named individual you do not know

---

86 Beware: specialized recruiters know a lot about your industry and will be aware if you lie or exaggerate.

▲ **DEALING WITH HEADHUNTERS**
Headhunters are the same as search and selection companies – they operate at the top end of the job market looking for candidates for specific roles. They will not see many applicants on a speculative basis, but a strong letter and CV should mean they will keep your details on file.

CANVASSING EMPLOYERS

Approaching employers "cold" is a highly speculative strategy – you have no idea if they are currently recruiting. However, if you can target the right employers with the right proposition, they may express an interest in meeting you.

 87 Include a career summary when making a speculative application.

Be polite to everyone you speak to at a potential new workplace

Use trade magazines to identify potential employers

IDENTIFYING POTENTIAL EMPLOYERS

If you have conducted your career audit and set your career goals, you will be able to identify the employment sectors you would like to work in. A little more research will provide a list of potential employers: Most major employers will include recruitment information on their Websites, and business directories can also provide useful background information.

DEVELOPING A PROPOSITION

When writing to any employer, you need to decide exactly what you want to do for them – and then tell them precisely. It is no use sending a resumé with an "I wondered if you might be interested" message. You need to tell them you want to work as an *abc,* for *def* reasons. You are qualified to do this because of *ghi,* and you want to work for them more than anyone else for *xyz* reasons. Confidence, determination, and flattery are all bound into one. Do not be too pushy, since the chances are they will not be actively recruiting; but express your interest in arranging an exploratory meeting.

MAKING A PROPOSITION TO EMPLOYERS

Tell them what you want to do

Tell them why you want to do it

Tell them why you are qualified to do it

Tell them why you want to do it for them

88 State your goals, but do not limit yourself too much.

89 Keep a note of those employers who do not reply.

DECIDING WHOM TO CONTACT

The right proposition needs to land on the right desk. Personnel or Human Resources departments will be the gatekeepers for current vacancies, but you cannot rely on them forwarding your letter to the right line manager. The best course of action is to identify the right person yourself and write directly to them. If you want to work for the marketing director, write to the marketing director. Be careful not to aim too senior; it is the recipient you are aiming to see; you do not want your resumé – and you – to be passed down the line.

PROMPTING A RESPONSE

You should receive a polite acknowledgment to any letter you send. However, you cannot always count on it. When writing speculatively, consider saying that you will be making a follow-up call to find out if a meeting would be worthwhile. This demonstrates a positive attitude on your part, and may encourage a response.

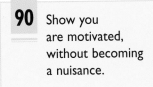

90 Show you are motivated, without becoming a nuisance.

QUESTIONS TO ASK YOURSELF

Q Am I using all the routes to a new job that are open to me?

Q Am I sending out the right sort of resumé to the right people?

Q Am I giving forms and questionnaires the same kind of detailed attention that I gave to my resumé?

Q Should I prepare myself for possible employer tests?

Q Am I coming across as highly motivated?

FILLING OUT FORMS AND QUESTIONNAIRES

Occasionally, an employer may respond with either an application form or a structured questionnaire – either is better than an outright "no." Take some time to read these carefully before starting to complete them. If the form asks you focused, open-ended questions, think about what the employer is trying to find out – for example, are the questions looking for detailed evidence of your transferable skills? Blank sections of forms that ask you to provide "any other information" are a further opportunity for you to sell yourself. Use the analysis of your transferable skills and your career objectives as the basis for your response.

91 Find the name of the person who can give you the job you want.

92 Ensure your career summary is no more than 50 words.

SELLING YOURSELF TO AN EMPLOYER

A sales letter is one of the most difficult business documents to write – and a speculative letter to a potential employer is precisely that. Your research may throw up opportunities, or recent press coverage may provide a lead, and an opening, for communication. Alternatively, start your letter with a powerful statement that headlines your own skills – for example, "Getting customers to pay on time is not easy, but I have spent 10 years doing precisely that." You must then summarize the key elements of your resumé and why you want to work for that particular employer. Close with a proposition of what could happen next.

A degree of formality shows respect for someone the applicant hopes may become their boss

Mr. S. Mayne
Financial Controller
Duke Fastenings

Dear Mr. Mayne

I drive past Duke Fastenings every morning, and I have heard from an increasing number of acquaintances that you are one of the best employers locally. So I have now plucked up the courage to see if you have a vacancy for a credit control supervisor, or, if you have not, then to ask that you consider me when you do.

As you will see from my resumé, I have considerable experience in making sure customers pay on time and have completed courses to gain relevant qualifications.

I would welcome the opportunity of discussing the matter with you, and to that end I will call your office next week to see if a meeting can be arranged.

Yours sincerely

cc. Ms. R. Knowles, Personnel Dept

◀ **WRITING A LETTER TO A LOCAL EMPLOYER**
The recipient of this particular letter is not necessarily an experienced recruiter, but he will be aware of the needs of his part of the company. The letter states clearly why the applicant should be considered for a specific post.

A good, positive, flattering start

It is unlikely that a job will be available and this sounds a realistic note

This shows an understanding of the most important part of the job and goes on to show initiative

It is clear that this is not a half-hearted approach

Sending a copy of an application to the personnel department is a courteous thing to do

An opening like this gives all kinds of positive messages. A real interest in your industry also implies a high level of commitment

Ms. P. Gates
Managing Consultant
PG Human Resources

Dear Ms. Gates

This strikes the right balance between being enthusiastic and realistic

Your recent success in winning the New Deal contract made impressive reading in the Human Resources Journal. In the course of my 10 years as an HR professional, I have followed the development of your consulting business and would like to express my interest in joining you, either now or in the not-too-distant future.

As you will see from my resumé, I have gained comprehensive experience within HR/Personnel management:

It is obvious from this bullet-pointed summary that the applicant knows exactly what skills and experience this employer will be looking for

- 5 years generalist HR experience at manager level
- Specialized knowledge of compensation and benefits
- Experience across 3 industry sectors
- Record of success in change-management situations

Although proactive, this is still polite and gives the employer a way out if they are not interested

I would very much like the opportunity to discuss my interest in HR Consulting with you. To that end I will call your office next week to see if an appointment can be arranged.

Yours sincerely

---

93 Keep copies of every cover letter you send.

94 Avoid using humor in your application – it may be misunderstood.

▲ FOLLOWING LEADS

This letter came about as a result of trade press coverage. Being aware of what is going on in your field will open up possibilities to you and help you to talk confidently at interviews.

DO'S AND DON'TS

✔ Do be patient, people you write to may be away or very busy.

✔ Do be specific about what you want to do.

✔ Do demonstrate your knowledge of a particular company and the industry.

✘ Don't be unrealistic, most people you approach will not be recruiting.

✘ Don't become despondent if you hear nothing.

✘ Don't become a nuisance.

USING THE INTERNET

The Internet, and specifically email, presents the fastest-growing recruitment medium. The Internet offers access to jobs worldwide; however, because it is such a huge resource, the career seeker needs to use it selectively.

95 Avoid using email for sending confidential information.

96 Use a spell-checker to detect spelling mistakes when emailing applications.

CHANGING PRACTICES

Although the Internet may be rewriting the way business is conducted in a number of fields, in recruitment the basic rules remain the same. Your next job will still come through a job advertisement, personal networking, or through your details being in a database. However, the Internet changes the way companies operate and gives you greater access and more opportunities to network.

LOOKING FOR JOBS ON THE INTERNET

TYPE OF SITE	HOW TO USE THE SITE
THE JOB SITE Job sites come in all shapes and sizes, specialized and non-specialized. Some are simply noticeboards.	The big recruitment sites will have thousands of vacancies across entire countries or continents. Begin by limiting your search by location and type of vacancy. Many have search engines to help you refine your search.
THE CORPORATE SITE These are specific to one company and are used as a promotional tool that may include current vacancies.	Increasingly, companies of all sizes are establishing Web sites. These sites are a good source of background information on a company. They may advertise vacancies, and you may be invited to leave your details at the site.
THE DATABASE SITE These are run by the large Internet-based recruiting companies. This type of site is on the increase.	At these sites you will be invited to complete extensive online questionnaires, which build a profile of your skills, that are then matched against employers' needs. You should also receive feedback on your profile.

USING EMAIL EFFECTIVELY

Email may be a great boon for its speed and simplicity, but be careful how you use it. Most email systems allow you to request a receipt to be sent back to you when an item is delivered, or opened and read. Since a job application is an important document, this is a sensible precaution, and because it is an automatic function, it requires no effort on the part of the recipient. Use the email itself as a cover letter – this remains the first thing a potential employer will see, so make sure that you take as much care writing this part of your document as you would if you were posting your job application.

USING INTERNET RECRUITMENT SITES

Select the sites most relevant to your job search

Register your details with them

Revisit each site regularly to check on any developments

Update your details every three months

Check you have attached the correct documents before sending your email

MAILING RESUMÉS ELECTRONICALLY

The safest way to send your resumé is as an attachment to your email message – make sure you know which word processing packages can be opened by the recipient. There are also different conventions in page layout – in the United States, 8½ x 11 in (21.5 x 28 cm) is the standard "letter size" for printing. Above all, avoid sending your resumé as a text-only email – your application will look just the same as all the others.

CREATING A WEB SITE

For those people who are able to conduct a very public career search, there is the option of making a resumé available on their own Internet site and posting details within various search engines. For most people, taking advantage of this option will require specialized instruction – nevertheless, it represents the ultimate in self-promotion.

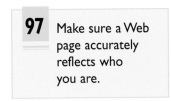

97 Make sure a Web page accurately reflects who you are.

KEEPING UP YOUR JOB SEARCH

For most people, a career search will last many months. You must be methodical throughout and weather both good news and bad. The whole process will take up a lot of time, but it will be an experience from which you will learn a lot about yourself.

98 If re-contacting, check your original contact is still working there.

KEEPING A DIARY

From the day you send your first job application, start keeping a job-search diary. Record what you sent to whom and when, and keep copies of job advertisements and covering letters. Having all this information at hand will enable you to keep track of responses received, as well as whom to chase. The diary will also help you to judge if it is time to make contact again, especially if you have received no reply.

Keeps a record of who has been contacted and when in a job-search diary

99 Try not to take the rejections you receive personally.

100 Prepare very thoroughly for all your interviews.

COPING WITH REJECTION

Every time you send a job application, you set expectations within yourself. However, more often than not you will have to cope with having those expectations dashed. The reality is that, no matter how suitably qualified you may be, there will be many others equally well qualified. Of all the qualities needed by the job searcher, persistence is the most important. The break you are looking for is that your resume obtains you a meeting. Every time that happens, you can celebrate a small victory.

RE-CONTACTING PEOPLE

Events move quickly for employers and recruitment companies, and memories are short. Using your diary, you will be able to monitor whom you have contacted, when, and what response you received. You may consider contacting a different person on a second attempt, or if you received a moderately warm response the first time, a mildly updated resumé can be sent after two or three months. Contacting the same organization every week is excessive, but a phone call every three months or so may increase your chances of success.

101 Celebrate every interview that your resumé earns you.

Remains positive throughout application process and at interviews

Prompted by job-search diary, phones to ask about progress of application

USING YOUR RESUMÉ AS A DEVELOPMENT TOOL

Even when you have completed your career search and landed a new job, make sure you regularly review your resumé. Set aside time twice a year to bring it up to date, identifying recent achievements, and any changes to your role. A well-kept resumé tells you how your career is progressing and helps to identify any areas that need developing. It will also make the start of your next career search easier.

Receives some rejection letters

ASSESSING YOUR SKILLS

This very simple questionnaire will help you to gain a better idea of what you think your skills profile might be. The most important part of this exercise is to discover the relationship between what you see as your strengths and your weaknesses. You must be honest with yourself; try to use 1 or 4, and only score 2 or 3 where you are in doubt. Your scores from this questionnaire will be used for the analysis of your profile on pages 68–69. The profile you produce may suggest new avenues for you to explore.

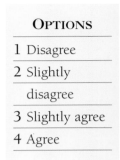

OPTIONS
1 Disagree
2 Slightly disagree
3 Slightly agree
4 Agree

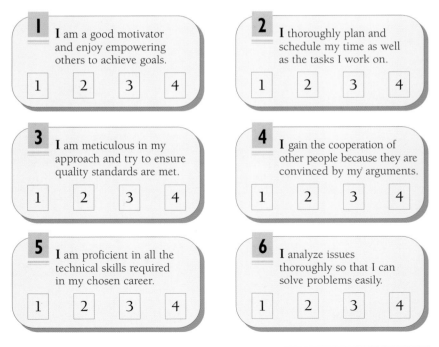

1 I am a good motivator and enjoy empowering others to achieve goals.

1 2 3 4

2 I thoroughly plan and schedule my time as well as the tasks I work on.

1 2 3 4

3 I am meticulous in my approach and try to ensure quality standards are met.

1 2 3 4

4 I gain the cooperation of other people because they are convinced by my arguments.

1 2 3 4

5 I am proficient in all the technical skills required in my chosen career.

1 2 3 4

6 I analyze issues thoroughly so that I can solve problems easily.

1 2 3 4

7 I speak confidently and clearly to both individuals and larger groups.

1 2 3 4

8 I write clearly and have been praised for my ability to communicate on paper.

1 2 3 4

9 I am driven by commercial principles and achieving the best value.

1 2 3 4

10 I am often ingenious in my approach and question traditional working methods.

1 2 3 4

11 I will often initiate projects and am always ready to make a decision.

1 2 3 4

12 I understand the wider implications and the longer-term impact of decisions.

1 2 3 4

13 I am sensitive to the needs of other people and work well with colleagues.

1 2 3 4

14 I adapt well to changing situations and respond quickly to changing needs.

1 2 3 4

15 I am stable under pressure and remain calm in the face of setbacks.

1 2 3 4

16 I work hard because I am committed to furthering my own career.

1 2 3 4

ANALYZING YOUR PROFILE

B*y plotting out your responses to the questionnaire on the previous pages, you will gain a clear picture of your transferable skills. This will enable you to emphasize your strengths and play down – or overcome – your weaknesses.*

CREATING YOUR PROFILE

To create your profile, photocopy the chart opposite or draw one up. Mark your answer between the numbers 1 and 4 in the first column according to your answers to the 16 questions on pages 66–67, then draw a line joining the marks. Look at the line; where it falls to the left it indicates your weaker tendencies, where it falls to the right it shows your stronger ones. In preparing your resume, focus on your strengths, since it is these that will get you your next job. By gaining a better understanding of your skills, you can gauge how best they will work for you. You will also need to account for your weaknesses.

▼ **ASSESSING SKILLS**
Your completed chart will give you a clear indication of where your strengths and weaknesses lie. It can also help you make the most of your skills and deal with any areas that you feel need to be improved.

CREATING YOUR SKILLS PROFILE

	1	2	3	4	SKILLS	DEFINITION
1					Leadership	Motivates and empowers others
2					Planning and organizing	Organizes events and use of time
3					Quality orientation	Ensures standards are met
4					Persuasiveness	Influences and convinces others
5					Specialist knowledge	Has good technical knowledge
6					Problem solving	Analyzes issues, develops solutions
7					Oral communication	Speaks clearly and fluently
8					Written communication	Writes clearly and concisely
9					Commercial awareness	Applies financial criteria to issues
10					Creativity and innovation	Creates new ideas and approaches
11					Action orientation	Makes decisions, takes action
12					Strategic thinking	Understands impact of events
13					Interpersonal sensitivity	Respects others and interacts well
14					Flexibility	Adapts well to change
15					Resilience	Remains calm under pressure
16					Personal motivation	Works hard for career goals

UNDERSTANDING YOUR WEAKNESSES

There are two ways of dealing with your weaknesses: you can either live with them or you can overcome them. Your approach will depend on whether the skills are integral to the work you may be taking on. The likelihood is that a number of your perceived weaknesses are in areas in which a possible lack of expertise will not adversely affect your prospects, or they may indicate a dislike for some particular tasks. Those things that you do not enjoy and are not good at are probably best avoided. The skills that you do need to fulfil your career ambitions need to be tackled through formal training or personal development. If it will improve your chances of success, enroll in a course or read self-help books that cover the skills you need.

CREATING YOUR SKILLS PROFILE

	1	2	3	4	SKILLS	DEFINITION
1	●	●	●	●	Leadership	Motivating and empowering others
2	●	●	●	●	Planning and organizing	Organizing events and using time
3	●	●	●	●	Quality orientation	Ensuring standards are met
4	●	●	●	●	Persuasiveness	Influencing and convincing others
5	●	●	●	●	Technical competence	Possessing the required job skills
6	●	●	●	●	Problem-solving	Analyzing issues, finding solutions
7	●	●	●	●	Oral communication	Speaking clearly and fluently
8	●	●	●	●	Written communication	Writing clearly and concisely
9	●	●	●	●	Commercial awareness	Applying financial criteria to issues
10	●	●	●	●	Creativity and innovation	Originating ideas and approaches
11	●	●	●	●	Action orientation	Making decisions, taking action
12	●	●	●	●	Strategic thinking	Understanding the impact of events
13	●	●	●	●	Interpersonal sensitivity	Respecting others, interacting well
14	●	●	●	●	Flexibility	Adapting well to change
15	●	●	●	●	Resilience	Remaining calm under pressure
16	●	●	●	●	Personal motivation	Working hard for career goals

INDEX

ACKNOWLEDGMENTS

AUTHOR'S ACKNOWLEDGMENTS

This book has very much been a team effort: I would like to thank Fiona Jobson and Geoff Thiel for their support, interest, and guidance. I enjoyed working with the team at Dorling Kindersley and would single out Gwen Edmonds and Laura Watson for their (almost) daily input and Stephanie Jackson for thinking of me in the first place. I would also like to thank SHL Group plc for permission to use their Inventory of Management Competencies, which was used as the basis for all references to transferable skills.

PUBLISHER'S ACKNOWLEDGMENTS

DK Publishing would like to thank the following for their help and participation:

Editorial Michael Downey, Nicola Munro, Jane Simmonds, David Tombesi-Walton, Sylvia Tombesi-Walton; **Design** Austin Barlow, Jamie Hanson, Nigel Morris; **DTP assistance** Rob Campbell; **Indexer** Hilary Bird; **Photography** Steve Gorton; **Photographer's assistant** Nici Harper.

Models Philip Argent, Marian Broderick, Angela Cameron, Kuo Kang Chen, Patrick Dobbs, Carole Evans, Richard Hill, James Kearns, Maggie Mant, Frankie Mayers, Sotiris Melioumis, Mutsumi Niwa, Kiran Shah, Lois Sharland, Lynne Staff, Gilbert Wu, Wendy Yun; **Make-up** Karen Fundall.

Special thanks to the following for their help throughout the series:
Ron and Chris at Clark Davis & Co. Ltd. for stationery and furniture supplies; Pam Bennett and the staff at Jones Bootmakers, Covent Garden, for the loan of footwear; Alan Pfaff and the staff at Moss Bros, Covent Garden, for the loan of the men's suits; David Bailey for his help and time; Graham Preston and the staff at Staverton for their time and space.

Suppliers Apple Computer UK Ltd., Austin Reed, Church & Co., Compaq, David Clulow Opticians, Elonex, Escada, Filofax, Gateway 2000, Mucci Bags.

Picture researcher Andy Sansom; **Picture librarian** Rachel Hilford.

PICTURE CREDITS

The publisher would like to thank the following for their kind permission to reproduce their photographs:
Key: b=bottom; c=center; l=left; r=right; t=top
PowerStock Photolibrary/Zefa: 31bl; **The Stock Market**: Jose L. Pelaez Inc 7r
Tony Stone Images: Bruce Ayres 4c; **Telegraph Colour Library**: D. Avuk 25tr; Masterfile 31cl.
Front cover **Tony Stone Images**: Bruce Ayres c.

The table of transferable skills on p. 17 is based on the SHL Inventory of Management Competencies and is reproduced by kind permission of SHL Group plc, who retain all rights in those works.

AUTHOR'S BIOGRAPHY

Simon Howard is a leading authority on recruitment. He has led a number of recruitment companies and been a director of the SHL Group, a leader in the design and publishing of psychometric tests. As well as writing the "Jobfile" column for the London *Sunday Times*, he contributes regularly to *People Management* magazine and has written on recruitment issues for television.